TUESDAYS WITH MORRIE

Mitch Albom

AUTHORED by Katie Logan
UPDATED AND REVISED by Bella Wang

COVER DESIGN by Table XI Partners LLC
COVER PHOTO by Olivia Verma and © 2005 GradeSaver, LLC

BOOK DESIGN by Table XI Partners LLC

Published by GradeSaver LLC, www.gradesaver.com

First published in the United States of America by GradeSaver LLC. 2011

ISBN 978-1-60259-251-3

Printed in the United States of America

For other products and additional information please visit
http://www.gradesaver.com

Table of Contents

Table of Contents

Biography of Albom, Mitch (1958-)

Mitch Albom was born in New Jersey in 1958, the second of three children. He grew up loving music and taught himself to play piano. In fact, throughout his teenage years, he played in bands. Albom graduated high school after his junior year and then attended Brandeis University in Waltham, Massachusetts, where he majored in Sociology. After graduation, he continued to explore the world and his love of music, performing in Europe and the United States. However, while living in New York in his 20s, Mitch took an interest in journalism and volunteered to work for a local weekly paper, the Queens Tribune. This piqued his interest in the craft, so he attended graduate school, earning a Master's degree from Columbia University's Graduate School of Journalism, followed by an MBA from Columbia University's Graduate School of Business. Never forgetting his musical roots, he paid part of his tuition by working as a piano player.

Following his academic career, Albom took on full-time writing, working as a freelance sports journalist in New York for publications such as Sports Illustrated and The Philadelphia Inquirer. He moved to Detroit in 1985, where he was a sports writer for the Detroit Free Press. He was able to use his talents in multiple forms of media, working in newspapers, radio, and television. He currently hosts a daily talk show on radio show and appears regularly on ESPN's Sports Reporters and SportsCenter.

Albom, who married Janine Sabino in 1995, is the author of four novels. Three of them have been turned into TV movies, including *Tuesdays with Morrie*, which was produced by Oprah Winfrey in 1999.

About Tuesdays With Morrie

Tuesdays with Morrie is based on the real-life relationship with author Mitch Albom and his college professor Morrie Schwartz. Morrie had been one of Mitch's favorite professors in college, and on graduation day, Mitch presented Morrie with a briefcase and a promise to keep in touch. However as time passed, distance and life kept the two from communicating.

One night, as Mitch, now a well-known journalist in Detroit, is watching a Ted Koppel interview on ABC, he sees his old professor as that night's subject. Morrie has been diagnosed with ALS, also known as Lou Gehrig's disease.

Mitch sees that his professor's time was growing short and realized he has not kept up his promise to keep in touch. He travels to his old professor's home and the two re-connect. The conversation is easy, as if no time has passed at all. Mitch promises Morrie he will be back. After another visit, he realizes that he still has much to learn from his old professor. They make a pact that Mitch will visit every Tuesday. Morrie agrees to let Mitch record these "final lessons" as the two discuss life, death and everything in between. The lessons from those Tuesday meetings make up the pages of *Tuesdays with Morrie*.

Character List

Morrie Schwartz

Morrie is a Sociology professor at Brandeis University. He connects with one former student (Mitch Albom) and during the end of his life, as he battles ALS, meets with him every Tuesday to discuss a multitude of life's topics. These Tuesday meetings become Morrie's final lesson.

Mitch Albom

Mitch is the author of the book, who tells the story of his meetings with Morrie. Mitch was a student of Morrie's, who promised to keep in touch following his college graduation. However, life happened and Mitch and Morrie lost touch. Mitch becomes a sports journalist in Detroit. After seeing his old professor years later on an ABC show, Mitch reconnects with Morrie. The two pledge to meet every Tuesday, where Mitch records the lessons he learns from his professor, years after getting his diploma.

Charlotte Schwartz

Charlotte is Morrie's wife. She collects the food that Mitch brings for the weekly meetings and gives Mitch updates on Morrie's health.

Ted Koppel

Ted Koppel is the ABC journalist and host of Nightline who did the original story on Morrie. This was the story Mitch saw that reminded him of his promise to stay in touch with his professor. As Mitch witnesses Morries deteriorating condition over the television feed, he realizes time is of the essence and he needs to get back in touch immediately. Ted Koppel and Morrie also form a bond, as Morrie is able to break down the hardened journalist's guard. The two become friends, and Ted does a 3-part series on Morrie, up until Morrie's death.

Connie

Connie is one of the members of Morrie's team of live in nurses. She is a good, compassionate friend to Morrie.

Morrie's Mother

We never learn her name, but Morrie lost his mother when he was seven years old. From this, Morrie learns that life can go on after a death.

David

David is Morrie's brother. He contracts Polio following the death of their mother. Morrie blames himself for this, as David awoke unable to move one morning, following a day of playing together in the rain. David spends his childhood with braces on his legs, in and out of a medical home. From his brother's disease, Morrie is able to learn compassion at a young age.

Charlie

Charlie is Morrie's father. He becomes hardened following the death of his wife. He came to America to escape the Russian army. He was uneducated, poor, and did not speak English well. Morrie was disappointed that he never experienced the feeling of love or warmth from his father. Charlie took Morrie to the fur factory where he worked in hopes that Morrie would make a career from it. Morrie absolutely hated it and vowed never to work in a factory.

Eva

Eva was Morrie's stepmother. She married Charlie the year following the death of Morrie's mother. Morrie received the love he longed for from Eva, a Romanian immigrant. She would sing to Morrie nightly, something he loved.

Peter

Peter is Mitch's brother. The two lost touch after Peter contracted cancer and wanted to fight the disease on his own, away from family and friends. Through Morrie's lessons, Mitch realizes the importance of family and is able to reach out and make a connection with him.

Major Themes

Relationships

Relationships are a big theme in the book. The relationship (past and present) between Morrie and Mitch, between Morrie and his caregivers, between Morrie and his family, and between Mitch and his brother all play a big part in the story.

Attitude

Throughout his illness, Morrie displays a very positive mental attitude. He does not feel sorry for himself because his body is slowly deteriorating. He looks at the positives in his life and the things he is still able to do. His positive attitude inspires Mitch and others in the story.

Purpose

As he reflects back on his life, Morrie realizes he purpose was to educate and he does it until the day he dies. This pushes Mitch to realize he is fulfilling his purpose in life (journalism) and the purpose of re-connecting with his brother.

Dependency

Morrie learns that he needs to depend on others as his body fails him. Mitch grows to depend on Morrie as well for life lessons.

Regret

Mitch states that he has regrets in his life, such as not reaching out to Morrie sooner or losing touch with his brother. Morrie almost seems to believe that there are no regrets, and that everything happens for a reason.

Devotion

Once they make the pact, Mitch doesn't miss a Tuesday with Morrie. He meets with him week after week, religiously. This teaches Mitch the importance of holding true to your word. Morrie depended on Mitch to make this visit every week, and in the end, Mitch depended on Morrie to be there to teach him.

Love/Compassion

Throughout the book, we see the love between Morrie and Mitch, the compassion between Morrie and his wife, the compassion between Morrie and his team of nurses, and the compassion as Mitch worries about his brother. There is even compassion between Morrie and Ted Koppel as the two become friends.

Mentors

Morrie was a mentor to Mitch in college and again later in life. The reader realizes the importance of having someone to look up to and guide them through life. Morrie was able to teach Mitch lessons up until his death.

Aging

Morrie teaches Mitch and the reader that there is nothing to fear with aging, and that it is all a part of life. He says everything comes in steps and you just have to face each step as a new challenge or opportunity.

Glossary of Terms

Amyotrophic Lateral Sclerosis

Amyotrophic Lateral Sclerosis (ALS) is an incurable disease of unknown causer where the body suffers from progressive degeneration of motor neurons in the brain and spinal cord. This leads to atrophy and eventually complete paralysis of the voluntary muscles. Also referred to as Lou Gehrig's Disease.

Atrophy

The wasting away of the body or an organ, due to nerve damage or defective nutrition.

Biopsy

To remove a piece of tissue from the body for the purpose of a diagnostic study.

Cue

A hint, imitation, or guiding suggestion.

Disillusioned

To free from or deprive of illusion, belief, and idealism, or to disenchant.

Exuberance

The act of being effusively and uninhibitedly enthusiastic.

Foundation

The basis or groundwork of anything.

Hibiscus

A woody plant, also called China rose from the mallow family. The hibiscus has large, showy flowers and is the state flower of Hawaii.

Inconsequential

Something of little or no importance.

Inherent

A quality that exists in someone or something as a permanent and inseparable element, quality, or attribute

Insidious

Operating or proceeding in a seemingly harmless way, but actually with grave effect.

Patriarch
The male head of a family or tribal line.

Peace Corps
A civilian organization, sponsored by the U.S. government, that sends volunteers to instruct citizens of underdeveloped countries in the execution of industrial, agricultural, educational, and health programs.

Prophet
A person who speaks for a god or deity, or by divine intervention.

Raspy
A harsh or grating voice.

Serene
A calm, peaceful, or tranquil state.

Sociology
The science or study of the origin, development, organization, and functioning of human society.

Subculture
The cultural values and behavioral patterns distinctive in a particular societal group.

Vengeance
The infliction of injury, harm, humiliation, or the like, on a person by another who has been harmed by that person; violent revenge.

Whimsical
To be extravagant, fanciful or excessively playful.

Short Summary

Tuesdays with Morrie is the final lesson between a college professor, Morrie, and one of his long lost students and the author of the book, Mitch Albom. After seeing his professor in an interview on the show "Nightline," the author is reminded of a promise he made sixteen years ago to keep in touch with him. Now stricken with ALS, Morrie does not have much time left, and Mitch recognizes this fact. He travels from Michigan to Massachusetts to meet with him. This meeting goes well and affects Mitch and Morrie so much that they meet for the next fourteen consecutive Tuesdays, up until Morrie passes away. During each of these meetings, they discuss a different topic about life. These topics make up the content of the book and include death, love, culture, marriage, regret and the world we live in, among many others. The reader feels many emotions while reading this book, ranging from happiness to sadness, and more than likely, will be wiping away tears at the end. It makes the reader think about their own life and ponder aging, forgiveness, family, compassion, and mentors in life, just as Mitch Albom does during the course of the book.

Quotes and Analysis

Do I wither up and disappear, or do I make the best of my time left?

10

This was the thought in Morrie's head when he received his diagnosis of ALS from his doctor. This is a turning point for Morrie as he has to decide how to live the remainder of his life.

The years after graduation hardened me into someone quite different from the stuttering graduate who left campus that day headed for New York City, ready to offer the world his talent. The world, I discovered, was not all that interested.

14

Many students upon graduation feel as though they can conquer the world. However, the world is already full of great talent. A degree in hand does not make you an immediate super star. You need to put in the grunt work and start at the bottom to make this happen. This tends to harden people and put a damper on their spirit or work ethic. This is something Mitch learns and feels upon his graduation from college. It is also part of the reason why he and Morrie initially lose touch. He is out in the world, trying to make something of himself and loses touch with the rest of the world. He needs to find a balance between his family and friends and the rest of his life.

After the funeral, my life changed. I felt as if time were suddenly precious, water going down an open drain, and I could not move quickly enough.

15

After attending his uncle's funeral, Mitch realizes that at some point, life does end. He realizes he needs to get his act together and move on with his life. It reminds him to take advantage of each opportunity and to foster good relationships with those around him.

He refused to be depressed. Instead, Morrie had become a lightening rod of ideas. He jotted down his thought on yellow pads, envelopes, folders, scrap paper. He wrote bite-sized philosophies about living with death's shadow: "Accept what you are able to do and what you are not able to do"; "Accept the past as past without denying it or discarding it"; "Learn to forgive yourself and to forgive others"; Don't assume it's too late to get involved.

18

This quote is a great example of Morrie's attitude. As he saw his time on earth ticking away, he wanted to make the most of it by reaching out and teaching others everything he knows. He realized the philosophies he has on life could help others, and he wants to get the word out to whoever will see his notes. His positive attitude in the face of death can help others to live a better life.

I traded lots of dreams for a bigger paycheck, and I never even realized I was doing it.

33

This quote shows that if you put your dreams on the back burner, you may make more money, but you might miss many things you would rather be doing with your time. You might not realize it, because you are enjoying the fruits of the bigger paycheck.

Well, for one thing, the culture we have does not make people feel good about themselves. We're teaching the wrong things. And you have to be strong enough to say if the culture doesn't work, don't buy it. Create your own. Most people can't do it. They're more unhappy than me - even in my current condition

35 -36

Our culture teaches many things that do not make people feel good about themselves. Images in the media can harm one's self image, for example. However, when it is in our culture, we believe it to be true. This can lead to unhappiness with one's self, as Morrie says here. He is dying, yet he is happier than most other people are.

So many people walk around with a meaningless life. They seem half-asleep, even when they're busy doing things they think are important. This is because they're chasing the wrong things. The way you get meaning in your life is to devote yourself to loving others, devote yourself to your community around you, and devote yourself to creating something that gives you purpose and meaning.

43

This is another piece of advice Morrie gives to Mitch. He notices that people are just walking through life, not taking the time to notice the little things. They chase bigger things such as money or maybe fame. He says that in order to find meaning and joy in your life, you need to love others, be a positive part of your community, and be something bigger than yourself.

Let's begin with this idea, Morrie said. Everyone knows they're going to die, but nobody believes it.

80

Morrie recognizes that while everyone knows they will die, they don't really think it will happen to them. Everyone's heart will stop beating eventually, but people feel they are invincible. This can mean two things: that people take too many risks and live carelessly, or that people do not take enough risks and live too safe a life, not enjoying each day to the fullest.

Be compassionate, Morrie whispered. And take responsibility for each other. If we only learned those lessons, this world would be so much better a place.

163

This was one of Morrie's final lessons to Mitch. He was teaching a lesson on compassion, saying that we all need to look out for each other. Don't leave someone in trouble. Do whatever you can to help someone. The smallest thing can make their world a better one. Moreover, they can pass it on and in turn, help someone else. If everyone was there for everyone, Morrie believed, this world would be a better place.

As long as we can love each other, and remember the feeling of love we had, we can die without ever really going away. All the love you created is still there. All the memories are still there. You live on - in the hearts of everyone you have touched and nurtured while you were here.

174

Morrie believes that love means immortality. Even if your physical body is gone, if people can remember the love you gave them, they will feel it, and you'll still be here in the form of that love. You will live on in their hearts and memories. So give as much love as you can when you are here. You will feel good at the time, and people will remember it long after you are gone.

Summary and Analysis of The Curriculum - The Audiovisual

Summary of The Curriculum - The Audiovisual

The Curriculum

Tuesdays with Morrie begins with author Mitch Albom summarizing and foreshadowing what the reader is about to read; his old college professor used the final months of his life to teach one of his old students all he know about the subject. The reader learns there were no books, but that many topics such as love, work, community, family, aging, forgiveness, and death were covered. Instead of graduation, a funeral would be held. The final exam is the book you are holding in your hands. The theme of the book is the meaning of life, which would be Morrie's final lesson to Mitch.

The book then flashes back to the author's point of view. The rest of the story will be told from his recollection of his relationship with Morrie. He goes back to the setting of 1979 at his graduation from Brandeis College. His tone takes a prideful swing as he remembers introducing his parents to his wonderful professor, Morrie Schwartz. As a thank you gift, Mitch presents Morrie with a monogrammed briefcase and promises to keep in touch.

The Syllabus

The foil in the book is not a person. Instead, the "character" that contrasts with our protagonist, Morrie, will be the disease of amyotrophic lateral sclerosis (ALS). This foil/antagonist will be Morrie's death sentence. He will not be able to partake in his favorite activity of dancing anymore, as his body will slowly deteriorate, starting with the legs and working its way up until Morrie suffocates. Morrie is told he has mere months to live. He ponders his life, thinking, "Do I wither up and disappear or do I make the best of my time left?" Morrie opts not to be ashamed of dying and to make the most of his final months.

He takes pills, attends therapy, and has live-in nurses for aid. He slowly starts to lose his ability to do the little things: drive a car, walk without a cane, go the restroom on his own. However, Morrie refuses to be ashamed to ask for help. His positive attitude draws a multitude of visitors. He holds a living funeral in his home, so he can hear what people have to say about him. He thought it would be a waste never to know their true feelings. From here, Albom foreshadows again saying, "In fact, the most unusual part of his life was about to unfold."

The Student

After getting the background on Morrie's diagnosis, the reader gets to learn about the other protagonist, the author, Mitch. He says after that college graduation day, he did not keep in touch with his old professor. This fact would be a conflict in Mitch's life, loading him with guilt. The 20-something left for New York City with a dream of being a famous musician, a piano player. However, for the first time in his life, he failed at an endeavor. The wakeup call of his uncle dying from cancer was a big part of the characterization of Mitch. He realized he was going to die eventually and needed something to show for his life. As a result, he went back to school and got a masters degree in journalism.

With this degree, Mitch took the first job that he was offered, that of a sports writer. He eventually took a job with the Detroit Free Press. He started to become very successful and make lots of money. He lived on a deadline. He got married after a seven-year courtship. He never had children because he was always working. He would think about his old professor, but never visit or call because he was too busy living his own life. He says it always would have been that way, had he not been clicking through the television channels one night.

The Audiovisual

Mitch comes across his old professor by a chance viewing of "Nightline" with Ted Koppel on ABC. Morrie had been writing his philosophies on life and sharing with friends. This story reached the Boston Globe, and a "Nightline" producer saw it in the paper, prompting a visit from Koppel and crew. Before doing the interview, Morrie had to "check Koppel out" and get to know him off camera. He was not star struck by the newscaster. He wanted to know his viewpoints on family, faith and his heart. He told Koppel he thought he was a narcissist. Nevertheless, he did the interview. During the interview, Morrie tells Koppel his biggest fear is not dying, but getting to the point where someone is going to have to wipe his behind.

Analysis of The Curriculum - The Audiovisual

The book starts out with a prologue to set the story up for the reader. This is done with the author, Mitch Albom, using a brief flashback to remark on his time with his old college professor, Morrie. In this prologue, the reader gets the first metaphor. This is of a pink hibiscus plant that is shedding its pink leaves. The plant is still beautiful, but is deteriorating, day-by-day. This is the metaphor for Mitch's time with Morrie as well. Morrie's health is deteriorating due to age and ALS disease, therefore so is their time together.

Time is a theme the reader will see throughout the book. Albom uses flashbacks in time to show his time with Morrie. Going back to their early time together sets up the story and helps the reader identify with the two protagonists. The reader can gain a similar appreciation of Morrie that Mitch does, because they get to meet him in his healthy stage, like Mitch, and watch his life wind down, also like Mitch. The technique that Albom uses here really ties the reader to the story and its characters.

The reader is also introduced early on to another theme of the story is the meaning of life. Morrie was a teacher until the end. He used the end of his life to teach Mitch about the important things, fully knowing that Mitch was going to turn the stories into a book (we later learn that he even helped pick the title). Through topics of culture, love, family, work and regrets, Morrie makes his final lesson the meaning of life. Each Tuesday, he presents a different lesson. This was probably done so that Mitch would have a full week to reflect on the teaching before moving onto the next one. Morrie knew that each topic was important and he wanted to give time to let each one sink in.

This book really only has one protagonist. This villain is not a human, but the disease of ALS that is making the end of Morrie's life difficult. However, one most consider what would have not happened if Morrie would not be stricken with this fatal disease. Mitch went to visit Morrie because he saw him being interviewed by Ted Koppel. Morrie would not have been the subject of an interview if he weren't sick, so Mitch wouldn't have seen him and become compelled to visit the professor. While the disease was bad, it was also the catalyst that reunited the teacher and student.

Characterization starts to take place early in the book. In the section **The Student**, the reader learns about Mitch's early adult life after college. This helps to develop his character as we learn how he lived his life and why he made some of the decisions he made. We learn he becomes a workaholic who tended not to focus on the important things in life. This development of his character helps the reader understand why Morrie's lessons were so important and needed.

Summary and Analysis of The Orientation - Taking Attendance

The Orientation

After seeing Morrie on television, Mitch realizes he is running out of time to keep up on his promise of staying in touch with the professor. He flies to Massachusetts and rents a car for the drive to Morrie's house. However, being a busy man, Mitch is not focused on Morrie during the drive. He is on the phone with a producer about a piece they were working on together. As he approached the house, he spots Morrie on the porch. However, he does not get off the phone, instead finishing his conversation before his sixteen-year reunion. This is a conflict for Mitch. Does he finish his job or spend every precious second re-uniting? Both are important to him.

When he finally gets out of the car, the teacher and student embrace in a long hug. Mitch recalls Morrie smelling sour, as people on medication tend to do. He is overcome with guilt, believing he is no longer the good person he was when he was a student of Morrie, saying he would stay in touch. He hoped to fool Morrie over the next few hours. Morrie sits down and takes his pills, then tells Mitch he is dying. Then he asks Mitch if he would like to know what it's like to die. Mitch says yes, and the first class begins.

The Classroom

Morrie tells Mitch he has become more interesting to people now that he is dying. He uses the metaphor of a bridge to describe where he stands in life: somewhere between being very alive and being dead. He says he is on his last great journey. Mitch faces an internal struggle at this point. He had been giving a warm welcome by Morrie, despite his lack of contact for sixteen years. Mitch constantly asks himself, "What happened to me?" He realizes he was too busy chasing a paycheck over the last decade and a half. This guilt will be a theme throughout the book for Mitch.

The biggest theme though, is about the student-teacher relationship from Morrie, and about how it continues. While teaching him about death in that initial visit, Morrie also teaches Mitch about culture, saying our culture doesn't make people feel good about themselves. We are teaching the wrong things. He says we need to create our own culture. He says this is a reason perfectly healthy people are unhappier than a dying Morrie: they feel they don't fit in with the culture dictated by society. This is a great characterization of Morrie, that even in death, he feels lucky. His character is developed by his statement: "I may be dying, but I am surrounded by loving, caring souls. How many people can say that?"

Morrie uses a breathing test to show Mitch how much time he has left. He compares each second of being able to exhale and speak a number to one month of being alive.

Morrie is able to get very few numbers out, saying his tank is almost empty. He is using "tank" as a symbol for lungs and life. Mitch promises Morrie he will be back to visit and hopes he will keep true to his word this time.

The book is full of allegories, short flashbacks to their college relationship or poems that represent stages of Morrie's life. These appear in between a multitude of chapters in the book. These allegories help the reader to understand the spectrum of the relationship between Mitch and Morrie or to show how Morrie might be feeling in his final months.

Taking Attendance

After their initial reunion, Mitch flies to London to cover Wimbledon. While on the other side of the pond, he is full of thoughts of Morrie. Seeing tabloids makes him think of how irrelevant this all is, while Morrie sits at home, deteriorating. He realizes what Morrie meant while talking about culture. Reading these tabloids will not make people feel good. Yet, this is how they immerse themselves. If people don't buy these things, they'll stop being printed and our culture will change.

Morrie had developed his own culture. He loved discussion groups, walks with his friends, dancing to music, reading, and writing. He loved to look at nature, not watch sitcoms on television. Mitch had also developed a culture or work, juggling multiple freelance jobs, along with his newspaper job. Seeing reporters chasing down celebrities reminded him of Morrie's saying that *people walk around with a meaningless life. They seem half-asleep, even when they're busy doing things they think are important.*

After Wimbledon, Mitch returns home to Detroit. Upon his return, he learns his newspaper union is on strike and his job was on hold. He was out of a job, out of his "culture." Mitch turns a corner and chooses not to see this as a negative. Instead, he realizes that there is an opportunity to change his culture and spend his time doing something worthwhile. He calls Morrie and they make plans to get together the following Tuesday.

Analysis of The Orientation - Taking Attendance

A foil is when a character has a contrast with another character, but in this story, Mitch has a foil situation with himself. He contrasts with his decisions, with his past self. He is ridden with guilt for not visiting his professor and for allowing himself to be so consumed in his work that he neglected his promise to visit his professor. The first time he truly feels this guilt is when he sees his professor on the porch prior to his first visit.

This also poses a dramatic irony. The reader knows that Morrie is going to be sick while reading about Mitch out covering sports stories around the world. Obviously a young Mitch doesn't know his professor will face this disease, but the reader does.

One wonders what Mitch would have done if he would have had a crystal ball into the future. Would he continue his workaholic ways or would he have carved out a day a year to pop in on his college mentor?

Earlier in the story, the metaphor is of comparing a dying hibiscus plant to a sick and dying Morrie. At this point, the reader gets another metaphor, this time from Morrie himself. Comparing life to a bridge, he remarks that he is standing at the end of his bridge, aka his life. This paints a mental picture for the reader of Morrie walking across the bridge, almost deteriorating as he gets to the end. We know he will finally crosses over out of this life.

Morrie uses his lungs as a symbol for his life. When he and Mitch do their breathing test, Mitch can count many numbers out on a single exhale of air. Morrie can get out much less numbers and those numbers continue to dwindle by the day. As the lungs start to let him do less, he knows he has less time to live. To Morrie, his lungs represent an hourglass with the sand nearly completely drained to the bottom half.

In this section, Morrie teaches Mitch about culture and how people develop their own. The example of this is Mitch in London seeing the tabloid magazines and realizing people have made this our culture. There is an allegory to this culture lesson as it can be applied further to Mitch's life. Mitch has developed his own culture of making work his life. Because of this, it has caused him to miss out on other things (such as having children).

Summary and Analysis of The First Tuesday - The Third Tuesday

The First Tuesday We Talk About the World

Mitch is greeted at Morrie's door by his nurse, Connie, who plays a big role in Morrie's day-to-day life. Mitch greets both Connie and Morrie, saying he brought a deli lunch from the grocery store. Morrie brings up the Koppel interview as they begin their discussion. He reminds his pupil that his biggest fear is having someone wipe his behind and that he knows that day is coming. He fears it because it is a sign of dependency. However, he'll try and enjoy the process, that it means he gets to be babied one more time in his life.

Mitch notices a stack of newspapers. He asks Morrie why he continues to read them. Morrie says that just because he is dying it doesn't mean he doesn't want to know what else is going on in the world. He feels more compassion for people suffering around the world, because he is suffering too. People suffering in Bosnia make him cry. He cries talking about it, saying he cries all the time now about other people. He notices that Mitch isn't ok with men crying and says he's going to loosen him up and make him realize its ok to cry.

Mitch finds it ironic that they're holding this meeting on a Tuesday. He says many of his classes with Morrie were on Tuesdays, back in school. Morrie's office hours were on Tuesdays. Morrie tells Mitch this means they are "Tuesday People." Mitch reverts to Morrie feeling sympathy for those around the world. Morrie gives him the lesson, "The most important thing in life is to learn how to give out love, and to let it come in." They end their session with a promise to reunite the following Tuesday.

The Second Tuesday We Talk About Feeling Sorry for Yourself

Mitch reminds the reader he is flying 700 miles a week to visit a dying man. Nevertheless, he is glad that he's doing it, and he goes into a time warp each Tuesday they are together. He stops bringing his cell phone and does no business. He puts all his focus on Morrie as Morrie is doing for him. His nasty union situation back home makes his meetings with Morrie even warmer. They talk about life and kindness in the midst of all the fighting. Albom uses simile here, saying the meetings "felt like a cleansing rinse of human kindness."

Before his second visit, Mitch got a bag of deli food for Morrie. As he walked into the house, he noticed that the disease had progressed, that Morrie could not lift his arms past his chest. He would ring a bell when he needed assistance to use the restroom. Mitch asked Morrie if he felt sorry for himself. Morrie said he allows himself the early morning for sadness, then moves on. He looks to concentrate on the positives in his life instead. He says his disease is a wonderful blessing, because even though his body is deteriorating, he has been given time to say goodbye. "Not everyone is so lucky," Morrie says. Mitch then asks Morrie's nurse, Connie, to teach him how to move Morrie from his wheelchair to his armchair. He wants to be able to help his professor in any way he can.

The Third Tuesday We Talk About Regrets

The third Tuesday, Mitch arrives with the usual food and something new, a tape recorder. He says he wants to remember Morrie's voice, and he wants to be able to tell his story. The voice on the tape will become a personified version of Morrie long after he is gone. Morrie does not oppose this. In fact, he encourages it. He realizes he is wise and wants his story to be told. This discussion is about regrets and Mitch realizes he will regret not having these conversations saved. Morrie tells Mitch he has no regrets. He says though that people are too busy to think about regrets, that they are focused on more egotistical things: career, money, the mortgage, a nice car. He says they need to be pushed in the direction of reflection, that everyone needs a teacher. Mitch realizes this is exactly what Morrie is doing for him.

He decides he is going to be the best student possible. He makes a list of everything he wants to discuss in his remaining time with Morrie. He was on a search for clarity for his soul. Morrie said they could discuss anything. Mitch decides they will talk about death, fear, aging, greed, marriage, family, society, forgiveness, and what makes a meaningful life.

Analysis of The First Tuesday - The Third Tuesday

This section acts as an exposition that demonstrates that the journey of their meetings is beginning. The first Tuesday is the start of many days of lessons. Originally, he starts by just brining food from a local grocery store. By the third visit, he is bringing recording equipment as well. He is learning from Morrie's nurse the basics of caring for Morrie, such as moving him from his wheelchair. He will continue to learn more lessons about caring for Morrie as the weeks progress.

Mitch is really facing a conflict. He is spending money and time to visit a dying man, but is fortunate that union issues are allowing him to do so. He chooses to spend the money for travel and to spend his time visiting his professor because he knows it is the right thing to do and it is what he wants to do. He realizes that spending this time will allow him clarity. It will allow him to have a chance to revitalize a friendship and to shape his own future.

After these early visits, Mitch points out that they are meeting on a Tuesday. This is noteworthy, because it was the day they always had class together. In this context, it really is as if they are back in school. Morrie is continuing to teach, while Mitch is continuing to learn. Their relationship as teacher and professor has come full circle.

One would think the mood of these meetings would be somber as someone is dying. However, that is not the case. The mood is upbeat and positive, due to Morrie's outlook on life and death. He sees the dying process as a chance to be babied again. He will cry occasionally, but then get over it. Morrie strives to get the point across to Mitch that life is too short to be sad and he sets this example for his student in their meetings.

One learns early on that Morrie himself is a motif for a good life. The theme of how he thinks life should be lived is carried on throughout the course of the story. Even early on in Mitch's busy working days, one knows that is not how life should be lived. Morrie teaching Mitch the early lessons of not feeling sorry for yourself, practicing kindness, and not having regrets set the tone for the rest of the book. Morrie has many lessons, as he has lived a good life.

Summary and Analysis of The Audiovisual, Part Two - The Fifth Tuesday

The Audiovisual, Part Two

Albom makes three allusions to the three interviews that Morrie did with Ted Koppel and "Dateline." These three interviews put Morrie's death into three parts: diagnosis, progression and the end. Here we are at the progression. Morrie and Koppel need no introduction this time. They speak of their childhoods before the interview begins. Morrie doesn't use his hands to speak like the last time. He had trouble with certain pronunciations. Morrie says he doesn't despair though, because he is surrounded by loving relationships. He says he doesn't fear not being able to speak, because he can communicate just by holding hands. The love that passes between the hands will be enough. Morrie then goes on to read a letter to Koppel that he wrote to a teacher who had written to him. This letter brought back his mother's death, which although was over 70 years ago, still had an effect on Morrie.

The Professor

Here Albom flashes back to an eight-year-old Morrie, receiving a telegram from the local hospital that his mother was dead. Morrie had to translate, as his Russian immigrant father spoke poor English. He heard his aunts cry, "What will become of you?" and burst into tears. After the death, his father shut down, and his brother contracted Polio. Morrie's world was crumbling. He saw love again when his father re-married. He received kisses from his stepmother, who would sing to him. While her songs were of poverty and cigarettes, Morrie still felt love through the melody.

As Morrie became a teenager, his father decided he needed to work. Albom points out that the setting is now the Depression, and the family was desperate for money after the stock market crash of 1929. His father took him to the fur factory where he worked. Morrie hated that windowless building. He promised himself he would never work in a place like this, where the boss yelled at people as they worked away. He never wanted to work where money was made through the sweat and tears of others. This led into his teaching career, one where he could have a positive influence. This is another characterization of Morrie, as the reader learns why he chose his profession and why he was so caring. He knew exactly how not to treat people through these examples.

The Fourth Tuesday We Talk About Death

The reader now returns to the dying Morrie's house, and Mitch and Morrie are discussing just that - death. Morrie says, "Everyone knows they're going to die, but nobody believes it." We know our hearts will stop beating, but everyone seems to have a sense of invincibility. It seems so far down the road, that we don't dwell on it. Morrie says that if you prepare yourself for death, you can be more involved in your life. This is a Buddhist tactic, ask yourself if today is the day and if you died today, would you have been who you wanted to be and done all you wanted to do? He says learning to die is learning to live.

Morrie says he didn't talk of death before he got sick, saying he'd be the healthiest old man you'd ever meet. He was one of those people who believed they would never die. Facing death however makes you focus on the essentials and you see everything differently. For example, if you know you will die, suddenly your job might not seem so important. A walk with a friend might become your top priority. You might appreciate nature more. Morrie says he notices the trees every day now.

After being on "Dateline" twice, Morrie becomes inundated with letters from viewers. He and his friends and family would gather for letter-writing sessions, where Morrie would dictate responses to each letter. It was as if he were leading a discussion group, part of the culture he loved earlier in his life. Another lesson from Morrie was no matter what, to take time to acknowledge those who had reached out to you. Through these letters, he was continuing to teach.

The Fifth Tuesday We Talk About Family

As September rolled around, Morrie found himself not teaching in a classroom for the first school year in 35 years. However, he continued to teach his old student, Mitch. On that fifth Tuesday, Mitch suggested a discussion on family. Morrie surrounded himself with photos of the family around his house. There is a metonymy here, using the word foundation to represent that your family is the ground upon which you stand on. In a moment of allegory, Morrie quotes the poet W.H. Auden saying, “Love each other or perish.” He says his disease would be unbearable if he was divorced or childless. Friends would stop by, but it would not be the same. Nothing else will give you that devotion, including money, fame, not work.

Mitch reflects on his life. He has no children. Morrie says he's not trying to tell Mitch what to do, but in his mind, having children shows you how to love and bond in the deepest way possible. He says he wouldn't change this for anything in the world. Morrie then questions Mitch about his family. He had met his parents at graduation, but wanted to know about siblings. Mitch says he has a younger brother, but then changes the subject.

Mitch's brother was his opposite: he had blonde hair to Mitch's brown, he was the poor student to Mitch's good one, and he was the druggie to Mitch's sobriety. However, he was the favorite of the family. He moved to Europe after high school to enjoy a casual lifestyle while Mitch went to college. Their biggest difference was health. Mitch was healthy, while his brother contracted cancer. He chose to battle the disease in Spain, away from family, not wanting any support. He ignored phone calls, despite Mitch's pleas for a connection. Mitch dove into work as he could not control his brother's situation, but he could control his own. He says he was drawn to Morrie, because he would let him in when his brother would not. This is why he changed the subject when Morrie asked about his sibling.

Analysis of The Audiovisual, Part Two - The Fifth Tuesday

Albom alludes back to Morrie's interviews with Ted Koppel. Koppel is a minor character in the story with major implications. If it were not for his first interview, Morrie and Mitch likely would not have ever reunited. These interviews tell us a lot about Morrie and his state. He hardly seemed sick in the first one and questioned Ted himself at the beginning, but by the last one, when his health had taken a major downturn, they were like old friends. Morrie shows here that one should always ask questions up front and learn about someone before fully trusting that person. Morrie trusted Ted with his story and wanted to make sure he was trustworthy.

There is a flashback in this section to Morrie's childhood. By taking us back here, Albom really helps the reader understand Morrie. Using this characterization to develop the character of Morrie, the reader can empathize with him even further. This is because the reader sees a mostly sickened character as an active child, learning about how the world works and deciding what he doesn't want to do with his life. Morrie learned how not to act from watching his father's coldness and hostility. By going back to his childhood, the reader can begin to understand why Morrie is so wise and why he's teaching these lessons to Mitch.

There is foreshadowing throughout the book, as we all know that Morrie is going to die. However, Morrie takes this a step further by discussing death and saying you can't be afraid of it. This foreshadowing allows readers to think about their own lives. If learning how to die is learning how to live, one can then ask what they need to do to get the most out of their own life. Morrie's gift is that he knows how to do this. By talking about his impending death, he is trying to help others live a fuller life.

Routine is a big part of this book. There is the routine of the visit every Tuesday, the routine of bringing lunch (even though Morrie never eats it), and the routine of the lessons. However, one thing that is never routine are the lessons themselves. Morrie knows so much about life,that he can teach something different every week. Routine can be seen as a bad thing, because people might not be adding enough variety into their lives, but even with their routine, there isn't a negative. While they do the same thing each week, they deepen their relationship, lesson by lesson.

The discussion about Mitch's brother is also a foreshadowing. The reader can assume that the brother would not be mentioned unless he serves a purpose to the story. Morrie's family members shaped who he became. Now the reader has a chance to wonder how Mitch's brother affected his life. The two were separated by distance and an unwillingness to communicate on the brother's part. Nevertheless, one is led to believe that this will be discussed further and become an important part of Mitch's life.

Summary and Analysis of The Sixth Tuesday - The Eighth Tuesday

The Sixth Tuesday We Talk About Emotions

For the first time, Morrie's wife Charlotte greets Mitch at the door. She worked at MIT and Morrie told her not to quit her job because of him. She warns Mitch that Morrie is having a hard time, but that he would be happy to see him. Upon seeing Mitch's weekly offering of food, she smiles, but mentions he really cannot eat anymore, and that he is on a mostly liquid diet. Mitch says he wants to help, to bring something. Charlotte tells him he is bringing something; he is bringing a sense of purpose to Morrie. Neither Morrie nor Charlotte is getting much sleep as Morrie's nights become labored. She says she will go get Morrie, so they can have their meeting.

This is the climax of the book, where Morrie is struggling to survive his coughing fits. He has so much more he wants to say, yet the disease is really starting to take over his body. After a violent attack, he checks with Mitch to make sure the tape recorder is on. Mitch says yes. Morrie, with his eyes closed, says he is following another Buddhist practice of detaching himself. He says that he cannot cling to things, because nothing is permanent. One can experience things, but letting oneself be penetrated by these experiences is problematic. People get in over their heads if they fully enjoy every moment, so they shouldn't believe the highest highs or the lowest lows in life. It's like dying. People know it's coming, but shouldn't obsess over it.

After making his point, Morrie launches into another violent coughing attack. Mitch does the first thing that comes to mind, give Morrie a hard slap on the back to release the phlegm. The attack stops. After a brief rest, Morrie says he doesn't want to die in a fit like this. Rather, he would prefer to go peacefully. Nevertheless, if it happens in a coughing spell, he needs to detach from it and say, "This is my moment," and accept it. He says he won't let go yet though, because they still have work to do and he has more to teach.

Before a flashback on Morrie's life, Mitch asks Morrie in an allegory if he believes in reincarnation. Morrie says perhaps, and that if it were true, he would like to come back as a gazelle. He says gazelles are graceful and fast. Perhaps this animal is a personification of how Morrie would like his death to be. Graceful and serene, or if it is in a violent cough attack, hopefully it will be fast.

The Professor, Part Two

Morrie's character was shaped further after he received his Ph.D. He decided to do work for the world through research and received a grant to observe mental patients and make records of their treatments in Washington D.C. This was a groundbreaking study in the 1950s. He observed screaming patients, patients defecating in their underwear, refusing to eat, and needing to be held down. There was a woman who would lie face down on a tile floor all day. Morrie felt sorry for the woman and eventually would lie with her. He realized she just wanted someone to notice her. Through his time at the mental institution, he learned what most people needed was more compassion in their lives.

After working there, he started teaching at Brandeis University, which is where he and Mitch would eventually meet. This was in the 1960s. His sociology classes were popular. Morrie wasn't big on grades and gave students As so they wouldn't lose their deferment and have to go fight in Vietnam. He made friends with many students and many would tell him that they never had another teacher like him.

The Seventh Tuesday We Talk About the Fear of Aging

Morrie lost his biggest battle this week in that he needed help having his behind wiped. He accepted this and faced it head on. He taught himself to enjoy his dependency. He reveled in feeling like a child again. Through this, he explained to Mitch that it is important to live in the moment and find a positive in everything. He said it was fun to feel like a youth again. This leads to a discussion on aging. He said he didn't buy the emphasis on youth, that it's better to be older because you are wiser. He knows much more than he did at 22. He doesn't envy the youth though, because he can remember being that age and take himself back to remember the feeling of being any age he wants.

The Eight Tuesday We Talk About Money

Morrie says society puts our values on the wrong things. This goes back to culture. He says people lead disillusioned lives, that they are brainwashed that money is good and that what one owns determines one's self-worth. Morrie believes that these things are no substitute for tenderness or love, which becomes meaningful for him. He believes that love is the characteristic that makes people whole and happy. He says status will get one nowhere, but love will.

Analysis of The Sixth Tuesday - The Eighth Tuesday

When Mitch finds out Morrie doesn't eat the food he brings each week, he doesn't think he is helping his professor, but Morrie's wife Charlotte says that he is indeed helping, by giving Morrie a sense of purpose. Morrie knows he needs to stay alive each week so that he can finish his lesson with Mitch. The irony is that Mitch is probably extending Morrie's life, while he thinks he is just there to listen and be a good friend. In actuality, he is helping Morrie just as much as Morrie is helping him.

The climax of the book occurs in this section. Morrie is beginning to experience severe coughing fits that are literally killing him. He's taking a severe downturn in his health and his management of ALS. There are still more lessons to teach and the reader is left to wonder how much longer Morrie will be around to talk to Mitch. This is when Morrie's disease truly becomes real for Mitch, as he starts to witness these coughing fits and needs to assist Morrie, by hitting his back so hard that phlegm is released.

Morrie has a special place in his heart for Buddhism. While not a Buddhist, he uses some of the principles in his dealings with ALS. The theory of detachment is a big part what gets him through his coughing fits as he tries to detach himself from his body. This really shows the tone of Morrie's character. Even while going through something traumatic, he finds a way to get through it. Everything, even a cough, is a lesson. He does not dwell on things. Instead, he takes it for what it is and moves on.

When Mitch asks Morrie which animal he would like to come back as, he chooses the graceful gazelle. In this reverse of a personification (giving human qualities to animals), he takes the quality of an animal and puts it into the way he would like to be. The ironic thing is that Morrie appears to be quite serene. He handles things gracefully and takes them as they come. He already has some of the qualities of the animal that he would want to be.

There is another flashback to an earlier place in Morrie's life what Mitch delves into Morrie working at the mental institution. Morrie wanted to know these people and show them compassion, which parallels Morrie's life now. He has become the person that really needs the compassion and someone to listen. While not a mental case, his visitors have dwindled to just family and a few good friends, like Mitch. The mental patients were locked up and not getting visitors, but both need compassion. Morrie gave the compassion while he was there and is now receiving it from Mitch and his family.

Summary and Analysis of The Ninth Tuesday - Audiovisual, Part Three

The Ninth Tuesday We Talk About How Love Goes On

With each visit, Mitch notices Morrie sinking more and more into his chair. He asks Morrie why he will not lie in bed. Morrie's response is, "When you're in bed, you're dead." He says "Nightline" wants to come back, but they want to wait. This infuriates Mitch, as he feels they are exploiting Morrie, wanting to show him at his absolute worst. Morrie says that it is all right, and that he wants to get his word out to millions of people and this is his platform.

Mitch can tell that Morrie is tired. He asks if they should take a break from recording their sessions. Again, Morrie refuses. The professor says it is their last thesis together and they need to get it right. The topic becomes being forgotten after death. Again, the anthropomorphism of love comes back. Morrie says if people can feel love, they will feel and remember it. "It keeps you alive, even after you're gone," he says. He tells Mitch he wants his tombstone to read "A Teacher to the Last." Mitch approves, as this is very true of Morrie.

When speaking of love, Morrie is reminded of his own father. He did not feel much love from this cold man. In fact, his father died alone, of a heart attack after being robbed at gunpoint. Morrie was called to New York to identify the body. This helped Morrie prepare for his own death. He did not get the opportunity to say goodbye to his father or feel love, and he wanted those around him to experience these feelings before his own death.

The Tenth Tuesday We Talk About Marriage

The tenth week, on her insistence, Mitch brings his wife, Janine, to meet the professor. She had gotten to speak to him on the phone briefly, and wanted to meet the man who had captured her husband's heart. Morrie had remembered that Janine was a singer. He asked her to sing him a song. She did, and Morrie closed his eyes to focus on the notes. Maybe this reminded him of feeling the love from his stepmother when she sang to him as a child. By the time she was done, tears were streaming down Morrie's face.

On this Tuesday, they discussed marriage. Morrie says finding a loving relationship is so important, that people need a partner to take on the world with. They realize in tough times that they need someone who will do anything to help, like sit up all night with them like Charlotte does for him. Marriages are tested, and they help people figure out who they are. People need to respect each other. Again, he brings out his favorite quote: "Love each other or perish."

The Eleventh Tuesday We Talk About Our Culture

Morrie is really struggling by the 11th week, and Mitch needs to hit his back with a solid effort to halt the cough attacks. They make a joke about it, saying the hitting is for a "B" grade Morrie gave Mitch once in school, and that Mitch had been waiting for this moment. After the situation calms down, they discuss the good in people. Morrie believes all people were good and only get mean when they are threatened. He says our culture threatens people through things like the economy. He says the answer is not to run away, but to try to change it, as he did. He says even though people all have differences, we are really the same and need to learn to work together.

The Audiovisual, Part Three

Ted Koppel and the ABC crew come back for their third and final visit. Mitch notices the simile that this is more like a goodbye than an interview. Morrie and Koppel now refer to each other as friends. Koppel asks Morrie if he is afraid now that death is near. He says no, and that he is less afraid. He knows things are getting bad, and he does not want to live this way. As Albom says, “He told Koppel he knew when it would be time to say goodbye.” As the interview wraps, Koppel asks for a final lesson. Morrie says that people need to be compassionate and take responsibility for each other. Koppel is near tears as the interview wraps, telling Morrie, “You done good.” Morrie said he hopes so, and in his first reference to God, says that he is bargaining with Him to get to be one of the angels

Analysis of The Ninth Tuesday - Audiovisual, Part Three

Morrie and Mitch start to talk about death and being forgotten when you die. The concept of love keeping you alive comes up. Morrie thinks that as long as people remember how you made them feel, they won't forget you. This anthropomorphism gives a human touch to love. He is almost saying you can be re-born each time someone remembers you, because your love is still existing on the planet.

Morrie uses concepts from the arts many times throughout his teachings on life. Having Mitch's wife sing to him soothes him. He tends to quote poetry frequently. He reads books and the newspaper. Using the arts on a daily basis keeps him happy and content, as it is something he has loved for most of his life (as he used to be a frequent dancer when he was in better physical condition). All of these things tie back to love. When people hear the quotes from the poems or hear a song Morrie loved, they will continue to remember him.

Towards the end of his life, culture continued to be an important concept for Morrie. He believes people have learned to develop a culture of greed through economic issues. For a better world, he knows people need to work together. This is evident in Morrie's care. He has his wife, nurses, his sons, and Mitch all there for him. These people have become a hospice for him, creating a culture of caring by working together to keep Morrie comfortable. This is a strong example of the culture Morrie believes everyone needs.

The third and final interview with Ted Koppel also occurs in this section. This is also foreshadowing into Morrie's impending death. The crew had wanted to come at this point to show Morrie in a poor state, which Mitch didn't think should be done. The crew and Ted knew that Morrie's life was ending, especially as the two shared a somber goodbye at the interview's conclusion. The reader becomes aware that the end is coming soon.

There were three "audiovisuals" throughout the book. These show three different stages of Morrie's ALS. By doing this, Albom divides the book into three sections of his health, showing the decline as it progressed. This imagery helps the reader understand what Morrie is going through. It is entitled "The Audiovisual" because the reader can almost see and hear Morrie's voice through the way it is written. It sheds light on the different stages of a debilitating disease.

Summary and Analysis of The Twelfth Tuesday - Conclusion

The Twelfth Tuesday We Talk About Forgiveness

Three months into the time Morrie's final lecture began, he still sat in his chair. His feet were curled and callused. Mitch sat with him and rubbed his feet with lotion, as he had seen his caretakers do. Morrie pointed to a sculpture on the shelf that had been done by one of his old friends, Norman. Norman eventually moved to Chicago and when Morrie's wife had an operation, Norman never got in touch with them. Charlotte was very hurt by this and they dropped the relationship. Morrie refused to accept reconciliation with his old friend, due to pride, over the years. Morrie said just recently that Norman died of cancer and Morrie never forgave him. Not doing so pained him and was one of his biggest regrets. He told Mitch it is crucial to make peace with yourself and everyone around you.

Morrie and Mitch have a discussion of Morrie's death, more specifically his burial. He wants to be buried beneath a tree on a hill. He asks Mitch to visit every once in awhile, to come and talk, and all the better if it's on a Tuesday. Mitch says it won't be the same because Morrie won't be able to talk back. Morrie says this time it will be Mitch's turn to talk, and he will listen for a change.

The Thirteenth Tuesday We Talk About the Perfect Day

Morrie had decided to be cremated and in a joke with the rabbi, told him not to "overcook him." The rabbi was stunned, but Morrie could joke as he saw his body as a shell now, not himself. It was useless to him now, so it was easy to let it go. He says death is as natural as birth. He goes on to say that he has found peace with his situation, and that after a multiple hour coughing spell, he was ready to go. He said this feeling of acceptance is the most incredible and peaceful feeling.

At this point, Morrie points to a hibiscus plant. This plant is a metaphor for life, he says. Everything that is born will die. The plant was once beautiful, but now its petals are shriveled, just like Morrie's skin. They fall into the soil and help other plants grow. Soon, Morrie's body will be part of the soil too. However, humans are different from plants and animals because if others can remember the love we gave, they never go away andlive on through memories.

During this discussion, Mitch asked Morrie what he would do if he had one perfectly healthy day left. Morrie mentions waking up and exercising, having sweet rolls for breakfast and then going swimming. He would have friends over for lunch, one or two at a time so they could have a meaningful discussion. Then he would go for a walk and eat duck for dinner. The day would end with dancing and a deep sleep. A simple average day, full of the people and things he loved. He found perfection in the average, which according to Morrie's point of view was the whole point of life.

After this talk, Morrie mention Mitch's brother again. Mitch had been trying to contact his brother, but to no avail. Morrie tells Mitch he needs to be at peace with his brother's decision. Mitch struggles with why his brother does not want to see him. He says that he cannot dwell on it, and that he must focus on the positive times and give people what they want. His brother will find his way back to Mitch, just as Mitch found his way back to Morrie. Maybe here is where Mitch realizes the pain he caused Morrie by waiting sixteen years to reconnect. Now he is feeling this pain with his brother. However, Morrie welcomed him immediately, not questioning where he had been. This is the lesson he was passing on to Mitch.

The Fourteenth Tuesday We Say Goodbye

The fourteenth Tuesday, Mitch had a feeling that it would be the last before he arrived. Charlotte had called to say that Morrie was not doing well. He cancelled all of his appointments, except his meeting with Mitch. He arrived at the house and gave Charlotte a hug. When Morrie was ready, the student entered the professor's classroom for the final time. This time, Morrie was in a bed. The two held hands. He told Mitch that their relationship had touched his heart. Mitch called Morrie Coach, his old nickname for him, and said he didn't know how to say goodbye. They held hands and told each other they loved each other. Finally, Mitch said he would be back next Tuesday and Morrie snorted in a laughing tone, like he knew there wouldn't be another Tuesday. He kissed his cheek and walked out of the room.

Graduation

Morrie dies on a Saturday. He was blessed to have his family in the house, who sat by his bedside non-stop, sleeping in shifts around his bed. Morrie went into a coma two days after Mitch had left for the last time. The only time he was left alone was when the family slipped out to get a cup of coffee. When they returned, he was gone, almost as if on purpose, like he didn't want to haunt them with his final moment. He goes serenely, the way he had hoped. Morrie was buried in the spot he wanted, in front of a very small gathering, on a Tuesday.

Conclusion

Albom reflects on the person he was before being reunited with his old professor. He wants to go back to that person and tell him what to avoid and to look for what is important in life. He knows it cannot be done, but he knows it is not too late to change the rest of his life's course. He continued to try to reach his brother and was eventually successful. They had a long talk and Mitch told him he respected his distance, but wanted to be in his life as much as his brother wanted. For the first time, he told his brother he loved him. A few days later, he received a fax from his brother, with a few stories and jokes. The connection was made. Morrie was probably to thank for this.

Albom says the book, *Tuesdays with Morrie*, was Morrie's idea. This project, this "final thesis" as Morrie called it, brought them together. Morrie even came up with the title. Albom reminds his readers that they are lucky if they have a teacher in their lives that are even the tiniest bit like Morrie. He recommends trying to find your way back to them because one never knows how it could impact everyone's lives.

Analysis of The Twelfth Tuesday - Conclusion

There is one final flashback in the final section of the book. This time, Morrie looks back on his one regret, losing touch with a friend after fighting with him. The friend had died before reconciling. Again, these flashbacks, the good and the bad, help the reader to understand both Morrie and Mitch. They are fully developed because the reader knows everything from childhood to, in Morrie's case, death.

As the two discuss Morrie's burial, on a hill under a tree, Morrie asks Mitch to visit him. Morrie's soul will not be there, but his body will. This is another case of anthropomorphism, as human characteristics are assigned to a lifeless, cremated body buried six feet under the ground. Morrie still wants Mitch to visit him so that their talks will continue every once in awhile, although it conflicts with what Morrie said earlier. Technically, Morrie will always be with Mitch, no matter where he is, because of the love between the two men.

The metaphor of the hibiscus plant wraps up toward the end of the book. As Morrie is dying, so is the plant. It has lost its beautiful, pink leaves and is shriveled up. Morrie has lost his mobility and independence and is days away from death at this point. Both started out vibrant and bright, both would die, and both brought joy and beauty to those around them up until they died.

Mitch asking Morrie about his perfect day and getting a response about a normal day ties in all of Morrie's lessons. Morrie did not want an extravagant day. He did not need to fly to Europe and dine on the best foods. Instead, his perfect day would be spent in his community, with his loved ones. This really proves Morrie's point (and a major theme in the book) that love is vital and all one needs to be happy.

After Morrie's death, Mitch finally decides to get in touch with his brother. He likely would not have done so without Morrie's lessons about love and family. Even in death, Morrie played a big part in the reincarnation of a relationship. This is ironic because Morrie never met Mitch's brother or knew the details of why they were apart, but he played the biggest part in getting them back in communication. Even in death, Morrie continued to change the life of Mitch and likely that of many others that read the book and learned the professor's final lessons.

Suggested Essay Questions

1. **Did you have a special relationship with a teacher or adult? Explain their impact.**

   Here students can write about a special teacher, parent or adult in their lives. This can be someone who has made an impact on their lives so far. What lessons have they learned from this person? This can even expand into the relationship they hope to have with this person in the future.
2. **Have you struggled with finding your purpose in life? Explain.** Mitch had trouble finding a purpose in his life. Here, students can explain if they have found their purpose or if they know what they want to accomplish in life. Who are some examples of people who have found their purpose and have been successful in life that they wish to emulate?
3. **Morrie says everyone knows death will happen, but no one really believes it will happen to them. What are your thoughts on death? Do you feel invincible?** Youth tends to have an air of invincibility about them. Here, the student can discuss their feelings on the subject. Do they feel fear? Pressure to accomplish much in the time they have remaining?
4. **Morrie says he appreciates the small things in life, such as looking out the window at nature. What things do you appreciate and what do you think people take for granted?** One of Morrie's big points to Mitch is to appreciate the small things, such as looking at nature out your window. Here, students can discuss the small things in life that have meaning to them. Also, they can ponder ways to appreciate smaller parts of their lives.
5. **What is your perfect day and who would you spend it with?** Mitch asks this question to Morrie and his answer is a pretty plain day, with no extravagant plans. Here students will explain their perfect day and the person they'd like to spend it with.
6. **Morrie says there's no such thing as too late to do something in life. What would you like to accomplish? Is there anything that seems out of reach?** Morrie tells Mitch that no matter the age or the state of your life, as long as you're living, you can still accomplish something. In his dying days, Morrie was able to teach Mitch many lessons. Students may take the book and try to apply it to their own lives.
7. **Mitch wanted a connection with his brother. Why was this so important to him?** After Morrie pressed on about their relationship, Mitch was determined to get into contact with his brother. His brother was fighting cancer and Mitch realized he needed to check in. He realized the importance of this while he watched his professor waste away and wondered if his brother was suffering a similar fate, alone.
8. **Morrie was not a fan of the media and the images it portrayed to society. Why do you think he was so willing to let Ted Koppel and the ABC crew into his home?** Morrie wanted to show a real look at aging, not the glorified, plastic surgery look we tend to see. He says people are afraid

to get old. He shows that while it's not a field day, it's nothing to fear.

9. **The reader gets a brief look into Morrie's childhood. How did his relationships with his mother, father, stepmother and brother shape him into the man he became?** Morrie learned a lot from these people: death from his mother, how not to love from his father, how to love from his stepmother, and compassion and care from his Polio-stricken brother.
10. **Morrie had a hibiscus flower in the study where he spent most of his time. How does that flower relate or compare to Morrie's life?** This plant represents a circle of life. It started out young and vibrant, like Morrie, but as it aged, petals would wrinkle up and fall off. As Morrie aged, parts of his body would fail to work. They both live and they both die.

Tuesdays with Morrie - The Movie

Tuesdays With Morrie was turned into a made-for-TV movie, produced by Oprah Winfrey, although Morrie mentions in the book that he had only seen her show once in his life. However, his story inspired the talk show host, who decided to make a push for the movie, which aired in 1999 and starred actor Jack Lemmon as Morrie and Hank Azaria as Mitch Albom.

Morrie and Ted Koppel - Interviews

Morrie and Mitch were reunited because Mitch saw Morrie's "Nightline" interview on ABC. Over 10 years later, viewers can watch the actual Morrie and Ted Koppel interview, thanks to Youtube. By listening to Morrie speak, readers can feel even more connected with the professor.

http://www.youtube.com/results?search_query=morrie+schwartz+nightline&aq=f

Author of ClassicNote and Sources

Katie Logan, author of ClassicNote. Completed on December 28, 2010, copyright held by GradeSaver.

Updated and revised Bella Wang March 31, 2011. Copyright held by GradeSaver.

Schwartz, Morris S. Letting Go: Morrie's Reflections on Living While Dying. New York: Walker & Co., 1996.

Dictionary.com, LLC; Ask.com, LLC. "Dictionary.com LLC." Katie Logan. 2010-12-28. 2010-12-28. <http://Dictionary.com>.

Mitch Albom. "Mitch Albom." 2008-01-01. 2010-12-20. <http://mitchalbom.com/>.

Stephanie Bowen. "Books Reviews Tuesdays with Morrie." CNN. 1998-05-07. 2010-12-28. <http://articles.cnn.com/1998-05-07/entertainment/reviews_9805_06_1_disease-insight-profess

Scott Fabirkiewicz. "Scooter Chronicals." Scott Fabirkiewicz. 2009-09-13. 2010-12-28. <http://scooterchronicles.com/2009/09/13/have-a-little-faith-by-mitch-albom/>.

Youtube - Broadcast Yourself. "Morrie Schwartz's Interviews on Nightline." Amandalai4utube. 2007-10-07. 2010-12-29. <http://www.youtube.com/watch?v=DbcHxA55sek&playnext=1&list=PL2656BAC7D66B106

International Movie Database. "Tuesdays with Morrie (TV)." Amazon.com. 1999-12-05. 2010-12-29. <http://www.imdb.com/title/tt0207805/>.

Quiz 1

1. **Where did Morrie teach?**
   A. Brandeis University
   B. Boston College
   C. Amherst College
   D. Boston University

2. **What gift did Mitch give Morrie on graduation day?**
   A. A journal
   B. A signed yearbook
   C. His notes from Morrie's classes
   D. A monogrammed briefcase

3. **What was Morrie's favorite past time?**
   A. Movies
   B. Dancing
   C. Puzzles
   D. Writing Novels

4. **What subject did Morrie teach?**
   A. Biology
   B. Sociology
   C. Philosophy
   D. Pyschology

5. **Why did Morrie go the the doctor in the first place?**
   A. Couldn't lift his arm
   B. Headache
   C. Fell Dancing
   D. Stomach Pain

6. **What does ALS stand for?**
   A. Alzheimers Diesease
   B. Arms and Legs Syndrome
   C. Armstrong Lincoln Stevens Sclerosis
   D. Amyotrophic Lateral Sclerosis

7. **Which well-known athlete also contracted ALS?**
   A. Babe Ruth
   B. Jackie Robinson
   C. Lou Gehrig
   D. Barry Bonds

8. **What was the first struggle from ALS for Morrie?**
   A. Couldn't walk without a cane
   B. Lost ability to drive
   C. Couldn't swim at the YMCA
   D. Couldn't undress himself

9. **How does ALS kill it's victim?**
   A. Lose ability to eat or drink
   B. Muscles stop working
   C. Lose ability to breathe
   D. Organs fail

10. **How long do most people live with ALS?**
    A. 10 Years
    B. 5 Months
    C. 2 Years
    D. 5 Years

11. **How did Morrie entertain visitors?**
    A. Looking at old photos
    B. Reading through books
    C. Sitting outside
    D. Led discussion groups on dying

12. **How did Morrie choose to celebrate his life with friends?**
    A. He wrote the script for his funeral
    B. He didn't want a funeral at all
    C. He wrote his obituary
    D. He held a living funeral

13. **Where did Mitch go after graduation?**
    A. Boston
    B. Chicago
    C. Detroit
    D. New York City

14. **What instrument did Mitch play?**
    A. Guitar
    B. Violin
    C. Tuba
    D. Piano

15. **What was Mitch's first failure in life?**
    A. Didn't get into graduate school
    B. Couldn't pay rent at his first apartment
    C. Inability to be a famous musician
    D. Getting a C in Morrie's class

16. **What was Mitch's first encounter with death?**
    A. His uncle
    B. His father
    C. His mother
    D. His brother

17. **What did Mitch think he would die of?**
    A. Heart Disease
    B. ALS
    C. Lonliness
    D. Cancer

18. **What was Mitch's graduate degree in?**
    A. Creative Writing
    B. Journalism
    C. Drama
    D. Musical Production

19. **What was Mitch's first job out of Graduate School?**
    A. News Producer
    B. Sports Writer
    C. Custodian
    D. Public Relations Manager

20. **Where was Mitch a columnist?**
    A. New York Times
    B. Detroit Free Press
    C. Columbus Dispatch
    D. Tampa Observatory

21. **How many children did Mitch and his wife have?**
    A. 0
    B. 1
    C. 2
    D. 3

22. **Where did Mitch here of Morrie again?**
    A. 20/20
    B. Dateline
    C. Nightline
    D. Newspaper article

23. **Who interviewed Morrie for the television show?**
    A. Barbara Walters
    B. Ted Koppel
    C. Hugh Downs
    D. Katie Couric

24. **How did Dateline hear of Morrie?**
    A. Boston Globe article
    B. New York Times article
    C. Student in Morrie's class
    D. Mitch called the producer

25. **What did Morrie do upon meeting Ted Koppel?**

A. Was an excited fan

B. Ignored him

C. Questioned him about life

D. Read him his journal

Quiz 1 Answer Key

1. **(A)** Brandeis University
2. **(D)** A monogrammed briefcase
3. **(B)** Dancing
4. **(B)** Sociology
5. **(C)** Fell Dancing
6. **(D)** Amyotrophic Lateral Sclerosis
7. **(C)** Lou Gehrig
8. **(B)** Lost ability to drive
9. **(C)** Lose ability to breathe
10. **(D)** 5 Years
11. **(D)** Led discussion groups on dying
12. **(D)** He held a living funeral
13. **(D)** New York City
14. **(D)** Piano
15. **(C)** Inability to be a famous musician
16. **(A)** His uncle
17. **(D)** Cancer
18. **(B)** Journalism
19. **(B)** Sports Writer
20. **(B)** Detroit Free Press
21. **(A)** 0
22. **(C)** Nightline
23. **(B)** Ted Koppel
24. **(A)** Boston Globe article
25. **(C)** Questioned him about life

Quiz 2

1. **What did Morrie think of Ted Koppel?**
   A. He was a talented journalist
   B. He was friendly
   C. He was rude
   D. He was a narcissist

2. **How did Morrie dress for the interview?**
   A. Shaggy sweater
   B. Coat and tie
   C. Button down shirt
   D. Sweatshirt

3. **Why did Morrie come across as exuberant on TV the first time?**
   A. Hands moved excitedly
   B. Spoke with excitement
   C. Legs weren't shown
   D. All of the above

4. **What name did Morrie mistakingly call Ted in the interview?**
   A. Ben
   B. Jon
   C. Fred
   D. Teddy

5. **Why was Mitch capitvated with Morrie in the first class?**
   A. Morrie didn't sit behind a desk
   B. Morrie got students involved in the lectures right away
   C. Morrie asked if he'd prefer to go by Mitch or Mitchell
   D. Morrie didn't use notes to teach

6. **What was Mitch doing when he got to Morrie's house the first time?**
   A. Thinking about Morrie's classes
   B. Listening to music
   C. Finishing his lunch
   D. Talking on the phone

7. **How did Morrie react to seeing Mitch for the first time in so long?**
   A. Coldly
   B. Affectionatly
   C. Passively
   D. Standoff-ish

8. **What did Morrie want to discuss first with Mitch?**
   A. What it's like to have home nursing
   B. What it's like to have ALS
   C. What it's like to die
   D. What it's like to not work anymore

9. **What did Morrie do for his students during Vietnam?**
   A. Gave them A's so they would keep student deferments
   B. Encouraged them to protest the war on campus
   C. Encouraged them to dodge the war
   D. Encouraged them to enlist

10. **What nickname did Mitch have for Morrie?**
   A. Dad
   B. Coach
   C. Teach
   D. Champ

11. **How did Morrie think people saw him in his dying state?**
   A. As a calm and peaceful man
   B. With looks of fear
   C. With looks of pity
   D. As a bridge between life and death

12. **What did Morrie think about our culture?**
   A. That it's perfect the way it is.
   B. That we're teaching the wrong things.
   C. He didn't have an opinion on the culture.
   D. That it's improving

13. **How did Morrie predict how much time he had left?**
    A. An internet search of his symptoms
    B. A breathing test.
    C. His doctor's word
    D. He saw his father die of ALS

14. **Where did Mitch travel after his meeting with Morrie?**
    A. Detroit for the Stanley Cup Finals
    B. London for Wimbledon
    C. Dallas for the Super Bowl
    D. Cleveland for the NBA Finals

15. **What was Mitch reminded of in London?**
    A. Morrie's thoughts on sports
    B. Morrie's thoughts on culture
    C. Morrie's thoughts on love
    D. Morrie's thoughts on death

16. **Why did Mitch have so much time to visit Morrie after London?**
    A. They met via phone conversations
    B. His newspaper union went on strike
    C. He took a job at the Boston Globe
    D. He quit his job to make the visits

17. **What did Mitch bring for every Tuesday visit wwith Morrie?**
    A. Deli-type food from the supermarket
    B. McDonald's cheeseburgers
    C. Salad
    D. Pizza

18. **What was the one thing that Morrie dreaded about his future?**
    A. Having someone wipe his behind
    B. Losing his memory
    C. Losing the use of his arms
    D. Dying

19. **How did Morrie look at the dying process?**
    A. As a scary thing
    B. As a chance to pick on his nurses
    C. Getting to be a baby one more time
    D. As a chance to be re-united with his mother

20. **What did Morrie make sure to do every day?**
    A. Read Newsweek
    B. Watch Nightline
    C. Write in a journal
    D. Read the newspaper

21. **Who did Morrie feel close to as he was dying?**
    A. People suffering around the world
    B. His wife
    C. Ted Koppel
    D. The nurses

22. **What typically un-manly thing did Morrie want Mitch to be able to do?**
    A. Get Pedicures
    B. Cry
    C. Bake
    D. Get Massages

23. **What did Morrie say is the most important thing in life?**
    A. To learn howto give out love, and to let it come in
    B. To keep a journal for future generations
    C. To stay in touch with people from the past
    D. To remember the little things

24. **How did Mitch travel to see Morrie every week?**
    A. Airplane from Detroit
    B. Bus from Detroit
    C. Train from Detroit
    D. Drove from Detroit

25. **What time of day would Morrie allow himself to feel sorry for himself?**

A. Morning
B. Before bed
C. Afternoon
D. Noon

Quiz 2 Answer Key

1. **(D)** He was a narcissist
2. **(A)** Shaggy sweater
3. **(D)** All of the above
4. **(C)** Fred
5. **(C)** Morrie asked if he'd prefer to go by Mitch or Mitchell
6. **(D)** Talking on the phone
7. **(B)** Affectionatly
8. **(C)** What it's like to die
9. **(A)** Gave them A's so they would keep student deferments
10. **(B)** Coach
11. **(D)** As a bridge between life and death
12. **(B)** That we're teaching the wrong things.
13. **(B)** A breathing test.
14. **(B)** London for Wimbledon
15. **(B)** Morrie's thoughts on culture
16. **(B)** His newspaper union went on strike
17. **(A)** Deli-type food from the supermarket
18. **(A)** Having someone wipe his behind
19. **(C)** Getting to be a baby one more time
20. **(D)** Read the newspaper
21. **(A)** People suffering around the world
22. **(B)** Cry
23. **(A)** To learn howto give out love, and to let it come in
24. **(A)** Airplane from Detroit
25. **(A)** Morning

Quiz 3

1. **Why did Morrie think the way he was dying was wonderful?**
   A. It allowed him time to write in his journal
   B. It allowed him time to reflect on life
   C. It allowed him time to write the book with Mitch
   D. It allowed him time to say goodbye

2. **What nickname did Morrie have for his relationship with Mitch?**
   A. College reunion pals
   B. Tuesday people
   C. Coach and player
   D. Death talk buddies

3. **What was the first part of taking care of Morrie that Mitch learned?**
   A. Lifting him from his wheelchair to his armchair
   B. Handing him his cane to help him walk
   C. Helping him use the restroom
   D. Carrying him to bed

4. **What did helping Morrie initially make Mitch realize?**
   A. That Morrie's legs were useless
   B. That Morrie was helpless
   C. That time really was running out
   D. That Morrie really didn't need the help after all

5. **What did Morrie think of Mitch recording their sessions?**
   A. He didn't knowhe was being recorded
   B. He wanted someone to tell his story
   C. He thought it was morbid
   D. He was offended that Mitch suggested recording their talks

6. **Who does Morrie say we all need in our lives?**
   A. Uncles
   B. Friends
   C. Parents
   D. Teachers

7. **What did Mitch write his college honors thesis about?**
   A. Baseball
   B. Football
   C. His college experience
   D. Death

8. **What did Morrie and Ted Koppel discuss before their second interview?**
   A. How TV production works
   B. Their childhoods
   C. If they'd do a third interviewtogether
   D. The last interview

9. **What was different between Morrie's first two Nightline interviews?**
   A. He couldn't walk around his house with Ted in the second one
   B. He dressed up for the second one
   C. He couldn't remember his past in the second one
   D. He couldn't talk with his hands in the second one

10. **What did Morrie do at the end of the second Nightline interview?**
    A. Read a letter he wrote to a Nightline viewer
    B. Was able to walk Ted to the door
    C. Told Ted that was the final interview
    D. Listened to Ted read him a letter

11. **What early event still effected Morrie in a negative way?**
    A. His step-mother's treatment
    B. The death of his mother
    C. Being ignored as a child by his father
    D. His brother's Polio

12. **How did Morrie hear of his mother's death?**
    A. He read a telegram from the hospital
    B. He witnessed it
    C. He read about it in the newspaper
    D. His father told him

13. **How old was Morrie when his mother died**

A. 6
B. 7
C. 8
D. 10

14. **What did Morrie's extended family worry about after his mother's death?**

A. Will he remember his mother
B. How his father will treat him
C. What will become of him
D. If he can take care of his brother

15. **What disease did Morrie's brother contract?**

A. Cholera
B. Dysenteria
C. Polio
D. Cancer

16. **Where did Morrie's father emigrate from?**

A. Russia
B. England
C. Romania
D. France

17. **What were the songs Morrie's stepmother sang about?**

A. Flowers
B. Puppies
C. Love
D. Cigarettes

18. **Where did Morrie's father take him to work?**

A. The local school
B. Leather factory
C. Beer plant
D. Fur factory

19. **What religion's philosphy did Morrie believe about death?**
   A. Jewish
   B. Baptist
   C. Catholic
   D. Buddhist

20. **In what trait does Morrie think humans are deficient?**
   A. Spirituality
   B. Charity
   C. Honesty
   D. Love

21. **How did Morrie handle the letters he got from fans?**
   A. He didn't read fan mail
   B. Dictate a response to his sons
   C. Write them back himself
   D. Send a video message

22. **How many consecutive autumn's did Morrie teach?**
   A. 25
   B. 30
   C. 35
   D. 40

23. **What is Morrie's philosophy on family?**
   A. Always stay in touch
   B. Take equal responsibility
   C. Love each other or perish
   D. Never go to bed angry

24. **When was the first time Mitch saw Morrie cry?**
   A. When Morrie told Mitch he was dying
   B. When he talked about leaving his children
   C. Morrie never cried in front of Mitch
   D. When they were first reunited

25. **Where did Mitch's brother move after high school?**

A. Europe
B. Florida
C. China
D. Haiti

Quiz 3 Answer Key

1. **(D)** It allowed him time to say goodbye
2. **(B)** Tuesday people
3. **(A)** Lifting him from his wheelchair to his armchair
4. **(C)** That time really was running out
5. **(B)** He wanted someone to tell his story
6. **(D)** Teachers
7. **(B)** Football
8. **(B)** Their childhoods
9. **(D)** He couldn't talk with his hands in the second one
10. **(A)** Read a letter he wrote to a Nightline viewer
11. **(B)** The death of his mother
12. **(A)** He read a telegram from the hospital
13. **(C)** 8
14. **(C)** What will become of him
15. **(C)** Polio
16. **(A)** Russia
17. **(D)** Cigarettes
18. **(D)** Fur factory
19. **(D)** Buddhist
20. **(A)** Spirituality
21. **(B)** Dictate a response to his sons
22. **(C)** 35
23. **(C)** Love each other or perish
24. **(B)** When he talked about leaving his children
25. **(A)** Europe

Quiz 4

1. **What illness did Mitch's brother suffer from?**
   A. ALS
   B. AIDS
   C. Parkinson's
   D. Cancer

2. **Who supported Mitch's brother in his cancer battle?**
   A. Mitch's dad
   B. Mitch's mom
   C. Mitch
   D. No one

3. **Why wasn't Mitch with his brother during his fight?**
   A. They were never close
   B. Mitch was with Morrie instead
   C. Mitch couldn't afford plane fare
   D. His brother wanted to fight alone

4. **What did Morrie's wife do during his ALS battle?**
   A. She moved in with their sons
   B. She quit her job and was with Morrie 24/7
   C. She had already died
   D. She continued to work at MIT

5. **What did Morrie say both the dying and healthy need to do?**
   A. Keep an ongoing photo album
   B. Immerse yourself fully in everything around you
   C. Always look at each day as a new opportunity
   D. Detach themselves from all situations, good and bad

6. **How did Morrie want to die?**
   A. Serenely
   B. Coughing spell to experience it fully
   C. Surrounded by his family
   D. During a conversation with Mitch

7. **If reincarnation was real, what would Morrie hope to come back as?**
   A. A person
   B. A gazelle
   C. A dog
   D. A lion

8. **What was one of Morrie's first jobs after getting his Ph.D?**
   A. Working in a mental hospital
   B. Working in a fur factory
   C. Student-Teaching
   D. Middle school principal

9. **What did Morrie do at the mental hospital?**
   A. Restrained them when they got angry
   B. Emptied bedpans
   C. Observed patients with a grant
   D. Talk to their families when they came to visit

10. **How did Morrie feel when the day of having to get his behind wiped finally came?**
    A. He refused help
    B. He only let his wife do it
    C. He ignored culture and said "What's the big deal?"
    D. That day never came

11. **What was Morrie's philosphy on aging?**
    A. Youth is the best time of your life
    B. As you grow, you learn more
    C. You stop really learning after college
    D. Aging is terrifying

12. **What does Morrie think the media is brainwashing the country about?**
    A. You have to go to college to be smart
    B. You have to have it all to be successful
    C. More is good
    D. You have to be thin to be beautiful

13. **What does Morrie think people are substituting in place of love?**
A. Education
B. Appearance
C. Thier homes
D. Money

14. **What does Morrie say will give you satisfaction?**
A. Volunteering with various groups
B. Running yearly fundraisers
C. Offering others what you have to give
D. Making large monetary donations

15. **What was the significance of Morrie's hibiscus plant?**
A. Represented the circle of life
B. It was a gift from his wife
C. It was from his father's homeland
D. It reminded him of a family trip to Hawaii

16. **Why didn't Morrie spend his days in bed?**
A. His bed was upstairs and too hard to access
B. He didn't want to die in bed
C. He thought "when you're in bed, you're dead"
D. His bed was uncomfortable

17. **Why didn't Mitch want Morrie to do a third Nightline interview?**
A. He didn't like Ted Koppel's interview style
B. He didn't want Morrie to die on camera
C. He didn't like that they wanted to wait until he was in his weakest state
D. He thought all had been said

18. **What does Morrie say keeps you alive after you die?**
A. Journal entries
B. Donations
C. Love
D. Photographs

19. **What did Morrie want on his tombstone?**
    A. A Brave Warrior
    B. Tuesdays with Morrie
    C. Love is All There Is
    D. A Teacher to the Last

20. **Why does Morrie think people are always "running?"**
    A. They're trying to "find" themselves
    B. People are bad at being on time
    C. They don't know how to slow down their lives
    D. American's are too overweight

21. **How did Morrie's father die?**
    A. ALS
    B. Lymphoma
    C. Heart attack after being robbed at gunpoint
    D. Pancreatic cancer

22. **What did Morrie ask Mitch's wife to do at their only meeting?**
    A. Tell him the story of how she and Mitch met
    B. Sing to him
    C. Tell him why she and Mitch didn't have children
    D. Look at old photographs with him

23. **What does Mitch have to do to Morrie to help him breathe towards the end?**
    A. Hit his back, hard
    B. Carry him outside for fresh air
    C. Shake his sholders
    D. Put the oxygen tank tube in his nostrils

24. **When does Morrie say people get mean?**
    A. When they watch violence on TV
    B. When they are threatened
    C. When they are angry
    D. When they are stressed out

25. **What American news story was going on as Morrie died?**

A. Ronald Reagan was shot
B. O.J. Simpson Trial
C. O.J. Simpson Bronco chase
D. 2000 Election

Quiz 4 Answer Key

1. **(D)** Cancer
2. **(D)** No one
3. **(D)** His brother wanted to fight alone
4. **(D)** She continued to work at MIT
5. **(D)** Detach themselves from all situations, good and bad
6. **(A)** Serenely
7. **(B)** A gazelle
8. **(A)** Working in a mental hospital
9. **(C)** Observed patients with a grant
10. **(C)** He ignored culture and said "What's the big deal?"
11. **(B)** As you grow, you learn more
12. **(C)** More is good
13. **(D)** Money
14. **(C)** Offering others what you have to give
15. **(A)** Represented the circle of life
16. **(C)** He thought "when you're in bed, you're dead"
17. **(C)** He didn't like that they wanted to wait until he was in his weakest state
18. **(C)** Love
19. **(D)** A Teacher to the Last
20. **(A)** They're trying to "find" themselves
21. **(C)** Heart attack after being robbed at gunpoint
22. **(B)** Sing to him
23. **(A)** Hit his back, hard
24. **(B)** When they are threatened
25. **(B)** O.J. Simpson Trial

Quiz 5

1. **When did Morrie first admit to talking to God?**
   A. After the third and final Koppel interview
   B. At his first meeting with Mitch
   C. He never did
   D. When he talked about Buddhism with Mitch

2. **What day of the week did Morrie die?**
   A. Monday
   B. Tuesday
   C. Saturday
   D. Thursday

3. **What does Morrie say you need to do before you die?**
   A. Decide if you'd like to be buried or cremated
   B. Forgive yourself
   C. Get your affairs in order
   D. Pick a saying for your tombstone

Quiz 5 Answer Key

1. **(A)** After the third and final Koppel interview
2. **(C)** Saturday
3. **(B)** Forgive yourself

ClassicNotes

GradeSaver™

Getting you the grade since 1999™

Other ClassicNotes from GradeSaver™

The Spanish Tragedy
Spenser's Amoretti and Epithalamion
Spring Awakening
The Stranger
A Streetcar Named Desire
Sula
The Sun Also Rises
Tale of Two Cities
The Taming of the Shrew
The Tempest
Tender is the Night
Tess of the D'Urbervilles
Their Eyes Were Watching God
Things Fall Apart
The Things They Carried
A Thousand Splendid Suns
The Threepenny Opera
Through the Looking Glass
Thus Spoke Zarathustra
The Time Machine
Titus Andronicus
To Build a Fire
To Kill a Mockingbird
To the Lighthouse
The Tortilla Curtain
Treasure Island
Trifles
Troilus and Cressida
Tropic of Cancer
Tropic of Capricorn
Tuesdays With Morrie
The Turn of the Screw
Twelfth Night
Twilight
Ulysses
Uncle Tom's Cabin
Utopia
Vanity Fair
A Very Old Man With Enormous Wings
Villette
The Visit
Volpone
Waiting for Godot
Waiting for Lefty
Walden
Washington Square
The Waste Land
Where the Red Fern Grows
White Fang
White Noise
White Teeth
Who's Afraid of Virginia Woolf
Wide Sargasso Sea
Winesburg, Ohio
The Winter's Tale
The Woman Warrior
Wordsworth's Poetical Works
Woyzeck
A Wrinkle in Time
Wuthering Heights
The Yellow Wallpaper
Yonnondio: From the Thirties